Twent...
SONGS

ROBER

'Twenty Favourite' SONGS and POEMS by ROBERT BURNS

Selected by J·F·T·Thomson,
Hon. Sec., The' Burns Federation.

·

Calligraphy by Tom Gourdie'

·

with a foreword by
A·C·W·TRAIN,
President, The' Burns Federation

Shepheard-Walwyn

This edition © 1978 Shepheard-Walwyn (Publishers) Ltd

First published in this format 1978 by Shepheard-Walwyn (Publishers) Ltd,
60 Fleet Street,
London, EC4Y 1JU.

.

.

ISBN 0 85683 040 2

Printed in Great Britain
by R & R Clark Ltd
Edinburgh

This volume, containing some of Robert
Burns' best-known songs & poems, and
inscribed by one of Scotland's foremost
calligraphers, is a great tribute to
Scotland's National Bard.
The poet became world renowned because
of his beautiful love songs and his intense
sympathy with the natural world —
whether bird, beast or his fellow man. He
composed according to his moods & his
everyday experiences. His works have
been translated into very many foreign
languages, including Japanese & Russian.
Tom Gourdie's expertise in handwriting
is likewise recognised not only in Scotland
but also further afield.
One only needs to examine any of Robert
Burns' original manuscripts to realise that
he, too, took a great pride in his penmanship,
and there can be little doubt that he would
have been proud, indeed, to know that his
best-loved works had been presented in
the style of this handsome book.

CONTENTS

My Luve'is like'a red, red rose,
  That's newly sprung in June';
My Luve'is like'the'melodie,'
  That's sweetly play'd in tune.'

As fair art thou, my bonie'lass,
  So deep in luve'am I;
And I will luve'thee still,my Dear,
  Till a'the seas gang dry.

Till a'the'seas gang dry,my Dear,
  And the rocks melt wi the'sun;
And I will luve thee'still,my Dear,
  While'the'sands o'life'shall run.

And fare-thee-weel, my only Luve'!
  And fare-thee-weel, a while'!
And I will come'again, my Luve,
  Tho' 'twere'ten thousand mile'!

MARY MORISON

O Mary, at thy window be,
  It is the'wish'd, the trysted hour!
  Those'smiles and glances let me see,
  That make the'miser's treasure poor:
  How blythely wad I bide the'stoure,
  A weary slave frae sun to sun,
  Could I the'rich reward secure,
    The lovely Mary Morison.

Yestreen, when to the trembling
        string
  The'dance'gaed thro'the'lighted ha',
  To thee my fancy took its wing
  I sat, but neither heard nor saw:
  Tho'this was fair, and that was braw,
  And yon the toast of a'the'town,
  I sigh'd, and said among them a',
    'Ye are'na Mary Morison.

Oh, Mary, canst thou wreck
   his peace,
 Wha for thy sake wad gladly die?
 Or canst thou break that heart of
      his,
 Whase only faut is loving thee?
 If love for love thou wilt na gie,
 At least be pity to me shown;
 A thought ungentle canna be
      The thought o' Mary Morison.

Ye' banks and braes o' bonie' Doon,
  How can ye' bloom sae' fresh and fair?
  How can ye' chant, ye' little' birds
  And I sae' weary fu' o' care'?
Thou'll break my heart, thou warbling
      bird
  That wantons thro' the flowering thorn
  Thou minds me' o' departed joys
  Departed never to return.

Aft hae' I rov'd by bonie' Doon
  To see' the' rose' and woodbine' twine';
  And ilka bird sang o' its Luve',
  And fondly sae did I o' mine';
  Wi' lightsome' heart I pu'd a rose',
  Fu' sweet upon its thorny tree'!
  And my fause' Luver staw my rose',
  But ah! he' left the thorn wi' me.

10

Thine' am I, my faithful Fair,
　　Thine, my lovely Nancy;
　　Ev'ry pulse' along my veins,
　　Ev'ry roving fancy.
To thy bosom lay my heart,
　　There to throb and languish;
　　Tho' despair had wrung its core,
　　That would heal its anguish.

Take' away those' rosy lips,
　　Rich with balmy treasure;
　　Turn away thine eyes of love,
　　Lest I die' with pleasure!
What is life' when wanting Love'?
　　Night without a morning:
　　Love's the' cloudless summer sun,
　　Nature gay adorning.

11

John Anderson, my jo, John,
  When we' were first acquent';
  Your locks were' like' the' raven,
  Your bonie' brow was brent;
  But now your brow is beld, John,
  Your locks are like' the' snaw;
  But blessings on your frosty pow,
  John Anderson, my jo.

John Anderson, my jo, John,
  We clamb the' hill thegither';
  And mony a cantie' day, John,
  We've' had wi' ane' anither':
  Now we maun totter down, John,
  And hand in hand we'll go,
  And sleep thegither at the' foot,
  John Anderson, my jo.

TO MARY IN HEAVEN

Thou ling'ring star, with less'ning ray,
  Thou lov'st to greet the early morn,
  Again thou usher'st in the day
  My Mary from my soul was torn.
  O Mary! dear departed shade!
  Where is thy place of blissful rest?
  See'st thou thy lover lowly laid?
  Hear'st thou the groans that rend his breast?

That sacred hour can I forget?
  Can I forget the hallow'd grove,
  Where, by the winding Ayr we met,
  To live one day of parting love?
  Eternity can not efface
  Those records dear of transports past,
  Thy image at our last embrace,
  Ah! little thought we 'twas our last!

Ayr, gurgling, kiss'd his pebbled shore,
  O'erhung with wild-woods, thickening
            green ;
  The fragrant birch & hawthorn hoar,
  'Twin'd amorous round the raptur'd
            scene :
  The flowers sprang wanton to be prest,
  The birds sang love on every spray ;
  Till soon, too soon, the glowing west,
  Proclaim'd the speed of wingèd day.

Still o'er these scenes my mem'ry wakes,
  And fondly broods with miser-care ;
  Time but th'impression stronger makes,
  As streams their channels deeper wear.
  My Mary ! dear departed shade !
  Where is thy place of blissful rest ?
  See'st thou thy lover lowly laid ?
  Hear'st thou the groans that rend his breast ?

My heart is sair ~ I dare'na tell,
  My heart is sair for Somebody;
  I could wake'a winter night
  For the'sake'o'Somebody.
    O~hon ! for Somebody !
    O~hey ! for Somebody !
  I could range'the world around,
  For the'sake'o'Somebody.

Ye'Powers that smile'on virtuous love,
  O, sweetly smile on Somebody !
  Frae'ilka danger keep him free,
  And send me'safe'my Somebody !
    O~hon ! for Somebody !
    O~hey ! for Somebody !
  I wad do ~ what wad I not ?
  For the'sake'o'Somebody.

15

Of a'the'airts the'wind can blaw,
  I dearly like'the'west,
  For there'the'bonie'lassie'lives,
    The'lassie'I lo'e best:
  There's wild-woods grow, & rivers row,
  And mony a hill between:
  But day and night my fancy's flight
    Is ever wi' my Jean.

I see her in the'dewy flowers
  I see her sweet and fair:
  I hear her in the'tunefu' birds,
    I hear her charm the'air:
  There's not a bonie'flower that springs
  By fountain, shaw, or green:
  There's not a bonie'bird that sings
    But minds me'o' my Jean.

TO A LOUSE – on seeing one on a lady's bonnet at church.

Ha! whaur ye gaun, ye crowlin'
    ferlie'?
  Your impudence'protects you sairlie';
  I canna say but ye strunt rarely,
    Owre'gauze'and lace';
  Tho' faith! I fear, ye dine'but sparely
    On sic a place'.

Ye ugly, creepin', blasted Wonner,
  Detested, shunn'd by saunt an'sinner,
  How daur ye'set your fit upon her—
    Sae'fine'a lady?
  Gae'somewhere'else, & seek your dinner
    On some'poor body.

Swith! in some'beggar's haffet squattle'
  Wi'ither kindred, jumping cattle';

17

There 'ye may creep, & sprawle & sprattle,
In shoals and nations;
Whaur horn nor bane 'ne'er daur
unsettle
Your thick plantations

Now haud you there, ye're 'out o'sight,
Below the 'fatt 'rels, snug and tight
Na, faith ye yet! ye'll no be 'right,
Till ye've got on it ~
The 'verra tapmost, tow'rin' height
O'Miss's bonnet.

My sooth! right bauld ye'set your
nose 'out,
As plump an'gray as ony groset:
O for some 'rank, mercurial rozet,
Or fell, red smeddum,
I'd gie 'you sic a hearty dose 'o't
Wad dress your droddum.

18

I wad na been surpris'd to spy
   You on an auld wife's flannen toy;
   Or aiblins some' bit duddie' boy,
         On's wyliecoat;
   But Miss's fine' Lunardi! fye'!
      How daur ye' do't?

O Jenny, dinna toss your head,
   An' set your beauties a' abroad!
   Ye little' ken what cursed speed
        The' blastie's makin':
   Thae' winks an' finger-ends, I dread,
      Are' notice' takin'.

O wad some' Power the' giftie' gie' us
   To see oursels as ithers see us!
   It wad frae' mony a blunder free us,
        An' foolish notion;
   What airs in dress an' gait wad lea'e us,
      An' ev'n devotion.

Is there' for honest Poverty
   That hings his head, an' a' that ;
   The' coward slave — we pass him by,
   We dare be poor for a' that !
   For a' that, an' a' that,
    Our toils obscure' an' a' that,
   The' rank is but the' guinea's stamp,
   The Man's the' gowd for a' that.

What though on hamely fare' we' dine,
   Wear hoddin gray, an' a' that ;
   Gie fools their silks, & knaves their wine,
   A Man's a Man for a' that :
   For a' that , an' a' that,
   Their tinsel show, an' a' that ;
   The honest man, tho' e'er sae' poor,
   Is king o' men for a' that.

Ye see'yon birkie'ca'd 'a lord,'
  Wha struts, an'stares, an'a'that;
  Tho' hundreds worship at his word,
  He's but a coof for a'that:
  For a' that, an' a' that,
  His ribband, star, an'a' that;
  The man o' independent mind
  He looks an'laughs at a' that.

A prince'can mak a belted knight,
  A marquis, duke, an a' that;
  But an honest man's aboon his
        might,
  Gude faith, he mauna fa'that!
  For a' that, an a' that,
  Their dignities, an'a' that;
  The pith o'sense, an'pride o'
        worth,
  Are higher rank than a' that.

21

Then let us pray that come it may
    (As come it will for a' that),
    That Sense' and Worth o'er a'
        the' earth,
    Shall bear the' gree' an' a' that.
    For a' that, an' a' that,
    It's comin' yet for a' that,
    That Man to Man, the' world
        o'er,
    Shall brothers be for a' that.

FLOW GENTLY, SWEET AFTON

Flow gently, sweet Afton! among thy
green braes
Flow gently, I'll sing thee a song in
thy praise';
My Mary's asleep by thy murmuring
stream,
Flow gently, sweet Afton, disturb not
her dream.

Thou stock-dove' whose echo resounds
thro' the glen,
Ye wild whistling blackbirds, in yon
thorny den,
Thou green-crested lapwing thy
screaming forbear,'
I charge you, disturb not my slumb-
ering Fair.

How lofty, sweet Afton, thy neighbour-
        ing hills,
  Far mark'd with the courses of clear,
        winding rills ;
  There daily I wander as noon
        rises high,
  My flocks and my Mary's sweet
        cot in my eye.

How pleasant thy banks and green
        valleys below,
  Where wild in the woodlands, the
        primroses blow;
  There oft, as mild Ev'ning weeps
        over the lea,
  The sweet - scented birk shades my
        Mary and me.

Thy crystal stream, Afton, how
lovely it glides,
And winds by the cot where my Mary
resides;
How wanton thy waters her snowy
feet lave,
As, gathering sweet flowerets she stems
thy clear wave.

Flow gently, sweet Afton, among thy
green braes
Flow gently, sweet river, the theme of
my lays;
My Mary's asleep by thy murmuring
stream,
Flow gently, sweet Afton, disturb not
her dream.

25

Scots, wha hae'wi Wallace'bled,
   Scots, wham Bruce'has aften led,
   Welcome'to your gory bed,
         Or to Victorie'!
   Now's the'day and now's the hour;
   See'the'front o' battle'lour;
   See'approach proud Edward's power—
         Chains and Slaverie'!

Wha will be'a traitor knave'?
   Wha can fill a coward's grave'?
   Wha sae'base'as be'a slave'?
         Let him turn and flee'!
   Wha for Scotland's King and Law,
   Freedom's sword will strongly draw,
   Free-man stand or Free-man fa',
         Let him follow me'!

By Oppression's Woes & pains!
By your Sons in servile chains!
We will drain our dearest veins,
But they shall be free!
Lay the proud Usurpers low!
Tyrants fall in every foe!
Liberty's in every blow!
Let us DO — or DIE!

Where' Cart rins rowin' to the' sea,
  By mony a flower and spreading tree,
  There' lives a lad, the' lad for me,
    He is a gallant Weaver.
  O I had wooers aught or nine,
  They gied me' rings and ribbons fine';
  And I was fear'd my heart wad tine,
    And I gied it to the' Weaver.

My daddie' sign'd my tocher-band,
  To gie' the' lad that has the land,
  But to my heart I'll add my hand,
    And give it to the' Weaver.
  While' birds rejoice' in leafy bowers,
  While' bees delight in opening flowers,
  While' corn grows green in summer
        showers,
    I'll love' my gallant Weaver.

TO A MOUSE *on turning her up in her nest with the plough. November. 1785*

Wee sleeket, cow'rin' timrous beastie',
   O, what a panic's in thy breastie'!
   Thou need na start awa' sae' hasty,
            Wi bickerin' brattle'!
   I wad be' laith to rin an' chase' thee',
            Wi murderin' pattle'!

I'm truly sorry man's dominion
   Has broken nature's social union,
   An' justifies that ill opinion,
            Which makes thee startle'
   At me', thy poor, earth-born companion,
            An' fellow-mortal !

I doubt na, whyles, but thou may
            thieve';
   What then ? poor beastie', thou maun
            live'!

29

A daimen icker in a thrave'
    'S a sma'request;
I'll get a blessin'wi' the'lave',
    An' never miss't!

Thy wee bit housie', too, in ruin!
    It's silly wa's the win's are strewin'!
An'naething, now, to big a new ane',
    O' foggage'green!
An' bleak December's winds ensuin',
    Baith snell an'keen!

Thou saw the'fields laid bare an'
    waste',
An'weary winter comin'fast,
An' cozie'here', beneath the blast,
    Thou thought to dwell —
Till crash! the'cruel coulter past
    Out thro'thy cell.

That wee bit heap o' leaves an' stibble,
  Has cost thee' mony a weary nibble'!
Now thou's turn'd out, for a' thy trouble,
    But house' or hald,
To thole' the winter's sleety dribble,
    An' cranreuch cauld !

But Mousie', thou art no thy lane,
  In proving foresight may be'vain ;
The best-laid schemes o' mice an' men
    Gang aft agley,
An' lea'e us nought but grief an' pain,
    For promis'd joy !

Still thou art blest, compar'd wi me !
  The present only toucheth thee :
But och ! I backward cast my e'e,
    On prospects drear !
An' forward, tho' I canna see,
    I guess an' fear !

31

O wert thou in the cauld blast,
　On yonder lea, on yonder lea,
　My plaidie' to the' angry airt,
　　I'd shelter thee', I'd shelter thee';
Or did Misfortune's bitter storms
　Around thee' blaw, around thee blaw,
　Thy bield should be my bosom',
　To share' it a', to share' it a'.

Or were' I in the' wildest waste',
　Sae' black and bare', sae' black and bare',
　The' desert were' a Paradise',
　If thou wert there', if thou wert there';
Or were' I Monarch O' the globe',
　Wi' thee' to reign, wi' thee' to reign,
　The' brightest jewel in my crown
　Wad be' my Queen, wad be' my Queen.

32

O Willie' brew'd a peck o' maut,
  And Rob and Allan cam' to pree';
  Three' blyther hearts, that lee-lang
      night,
  Ye wad na found in Christendie'.

    We are na fou, we've' nae that fou,
    But just a drappie' in our e'e;
    The' cock may craw, the day may daw,
    And ay we'll taste' the' barley bree'.

Here' are we' met, three merry boys,
  Three' merry boys I trow are we;
  And mony a night we've' merry
      been,
  And mony mae' we hope to be!

33

It is the moon, I ken her horn,
    That's blinkin'in the lift sae'hie';
She shines sae'bright to wyle us
        hame',
    But, by my sooth, she'll wait a wee'!

Wha first shall rise to gang awa',
    A cuckold, coward loun is he'!
    Wha first beside'his chair shall fa',
    He is the'King amang us three'.

    We are na fou, we're nae'that fou,
    But just a drappie'in our e'e;
    The cock may craw, the day may
        daw,
    And ay we'll taste the barley
        bree'.

As I gaed down the' water-side',
　There' I met my shepherd lad:
　He row'd me's weetly in his plaid,
　　An' ca'd me' his dearie'.

　　Ca' the yowes to the knowes,
　　Ca' them where' the heather grows,
　　Ca' them where' the' burnie' rowes,
　　　My bonie' dearie'.

Will ye' gang down the water-side',
　And see' the' waves sae' sweetly glide'
　Beneath the' hazels spreading wide',
　　The moon it shines fu' clearly.

Ye sall get gowns & ribbons meet,
　Cauf-leather shoon upon your feet,
　And in my arms thou'lt lie'& sleep,
　　An' ay sall be my dearie'.

35

If ye'll but stand to what ye've
    said,
    I'se' gang wi' thee', my shepherd lad,
    And ye may row me' in your plaid,
    And I sall be' your dearie.'

While' waters wimple' to the' sea,
    While' day blinks in the lift sae hie',
    Till clay-cauld death sall blin'
       my e'e,
    Ye sall be my dearie.'

    Ca' the yowes to the' knowes,
    Ca' them where' the heather grows,
    Ca' them where the' burnie' rowes,
      My bonie' dearie.'

RANTIN', ROVIN' ROBIN

There' was a lad was born in Kyle,
But whatna day o' whatna style,
I doubt it's hardly worth the' while
   To be sae nice' wi' Robin.

  Robin was a rovin' boy,
  Rantin', rovin', rantin', rovin',
  Robin was a rovin' boy,
  Rantin, rovin' Robin!

Our monarch's hindmost year but
   ane'
  Was five'-and-twenty days begun,
'Twas then a blast o' Janwar' win'
   Blew hansel in on Robin.

The' gossip keekit in his loof,
  Quo' scho, 'Wha lives will see' the' proof,
This waly boy will be nae' coof:
   I think we'll ca' him Robin'.

37

'He'll hae'misfortunes great an'
sma',
But ay a heart aboon them a',
He'll be a credit till us a' —
We'll a' be proud o' Robin.

But sure'as three'times three'
mak nine,'
I see by ilka score'and line,'
This chap will dearly like our kin,'
So leeze'me'on thee'! Robin.

Robin was a rovin' boy,
Rantin', rovin', rantin', rovin',
Robin was a rovin' boy,
Rantin',
       rovin'
          Robin !

Ae fond kiss, and then we sever;
  Ae fareweel, and then forever!
  Deep in heart-wrung tears I'll pledge
      thee,
  Warring sighs & groans I'll wage thee,
  Who shall say that Fortune grieves him,
  While the star of hope she leaves him ?
  Me, nae cheerful twinkle lights me;
  Dark despair around benights me.

I'll ne'er blame my partial fancy,
  Naething could resist my Nancy:
  But to see her was to love her;
  Love but her, and love for ever.
  Had we never lov'd sae kindly,
  Had we never lov'd sae blindly,
  Never met — or never parted,
  We had ne'er been broken-hearted.

Fare-thee-weel, thou first and fairest!
Fare-thee-weel, thou best and dearest!
Thine be ilka joy and treasure,
Peace, Enjoyment, Love, and Pleasure!
Ae fond kiss, and then we sever!
Ae fareweel, alas, for ever!
Deep in heart-wrung tears I'll pledge thee,
Warring sighs and groans I'll wage thee.

Should auld acquaintance be forgot,
  And never brought to mind?
  Should auld acquaintance be forgot,
    And auld lang syne?

    For auld lang syne, my dear,
    For auld lang syne,
    We'll tak a cup o' kindness yet,
    For auld lang syne.

And surely ye'll be your pint stowp!
  And surely I'll be mine!
  And we'll tak a cup o' kindness yet,
    For auld lang syne.

We twa hae run about the braes,
  And pou'd the gowans fine:
  But we've wander'd mony a weary fitt,
    Sin' auld lang syne.

41

We twa hae paidl'd in the burn,
 Frae morning sun till dine;
 But seas between us braid hae roar'd
 Sin' auld lang syne.

And there's a hand, my trusty
 fiere!
 And gies a hand o' thine!
 And we'll tak a right gude-willie
 waught,
 For auld lang syne.

 For auld lang syne, my dear,
 For auld lang syne,
 We'll tak a cup o' kindness yet,
 For auld lang syne.

Glossary

aft - often

agley - aslant

aiblins - perhaps

airt - quarter, direction

aught - eight

bane' - bone'

bauld - bold

bear the gree - take
    supremacy

beld - bald

bickering - hurrying

bield - shelter

big - build

birk - birch

birkie' - swaggering
    fellow

blastie' - blighted creature

brae - hill-slope'

brattle - scurry

bree - brew

brent - polished

but - without

cantie' - cheerful

Christendie -
    Christendom

coof - blockhead

cot - cottage

coulter - plough-iron

cow'rin' - cowering

cranreuch - hoar frost

daimen-icker -
    occasional ear of corn

daw - dawn

droddum - breech,
    rump

duddie - ragged

e'e - eye

fauth-ye-yet - confound you

fattrels - gewgaws

fause - false

faut - fault

fell - kill

ferlie' - a wonder

fitt - a song, strain

flannen - flannel

gaed - went

gang - go

gowans - Marguerites

gowd - gold

gree' - degree

groset - gooseberry

gude-willie' - goodwill

ha' - have

haffet - curls on the temple

hald - possession

hansel - first gift

hoar - snowy

hoddin-gray - coarse gray woollen cloth

ilka - every

jo - sweetheart

keekit - peeped

knowes - hillocks

laith - loath

lave - others, the rest

lave - wash

lee-lang - live-long

leeze' - blessings

lift - enduring

loof - palm

lout - stoop down

Lunardi - bonnet named after the balloonist

maun - must

44